Contents

Words that appear in **bold** in the text are explained in the glossary.

River wildlife

Let's go for a nature walk by the river. A river **habitat** is a good place to look for wildlife.

Listen carefully and you will hear
the sound of flowing water.

FRANKLIN WATTS

First published in 2010 by
Franklin Watts
338 Euston Road
London NW1 3BH

Franklin Watts Australia
Level 17/207 Kent Street
Sydney NSW 2000

Copyright © 2010 Franklin Watts

ISBN: 978 0 7496 9325 1

Dewey classification number: 577.6'8

A CIP catalogue for this book is available
from the British Library.

Planning and production by
Discovery Books Limited
Managing editor: Laura Durman
Editor: Clare Collinson
Picture research: Clare Collinson,
Colleen Ruck
Designer: Robert Walster, Big Blu Design

Photographs: FLPA: p. 9 (Richard Becker),
p. 14 (Roger Wilmshurst), p. 15 (Elliott Neep),
p. 16 (David Pattyn/Minden Pictures), p. 18
(Gerard Lacz), p. 21 (Roger Tidman), p. 22 (Phil
McLean), p. 23 (Derek Middleton), p. 26t (Tony
Hamblin); istockphoto.com: p. 6 (mikeuk),
p. 13 (EdmondterRiet), p. 25t
(WorldWideImages), p. 26b (JohnPitcher),
p. 27t (JLFCapture), p. 27c (Hans F. Meier),
p. 27b (adel66); Shutterstock Images: p. 7 (James
Bohn), p. 8 (Joe Klune), p. 10 (Elena Elisseeva),
p. 12 (hauhu), p. 17 (Dave Massey), p. 19 (Cynthia
Kidwell), p. 20 (Lobke Peers), p. 24t (Sally Wallis),
p. 24b (Sherri R. Camp), p. 25b (Nikola Bilic),
p. 28t (Photoroller), p. 28c (Planner), p. 28b
(jamalludin).

Illustrations: istockphoto.com: pp. 6, 11, 20, 26t,
26bl, (joaquin croxatto), pp. 8, 10, 26br, 27t,
29 (Hugo Lacasse), p. 12 (Bill Bartholomew);
Shutterstock Images: pp. 9, 22, 27b (Shaber)
pp. 14, 18 (Sceka), p. 16 (Shamzami).

Cover images: Shutterstock Images: main
(Christopher Elwell), top left (Lobke Peers),
bottom right (Rainbow).

Printed in China

Franklin Watts is a division of Hachette
Children's Books, an Hachette UK company.
www.hachette.co.uk

River safety

When you go for a nature walk by the
river, go with an adult. Take extra care
when you are close to the water. Do not go
into the river, even if the water is shallow.

Did you hear some quacks? There's a **mallard**, with her ducklings.

Let's see what other kinds of animals and plants we can find.

UP CLOSE

Ducklings leave their nests soon after they have **hatched**. They follow their mothers to the water and quickly learn how to swim and feed.

Ferns and flowers

Let's explore the **riverbank**. It is shady and damp here. What kinds of plants can you see?

UP CLOSE

As you walk along, look closely at the leaves of the plants you see. Ferns have feathery leaves called **fronds**.

fern frond

wild garlic

Where is that smell of garlic coming from?

It is coming from these wild garlic plants.
Many kinds of wild flowers grow along
riverbanks. How many can you find?

Reeds and trees

Look at these tall **reeds** swaying in the breeze on the riverbank. Reeds have soft white flowers in late summer.

UP CLOSE

A thick reed bed is a safe place for birds to build their nests and raise their chicks.

flower

Trees such as willows grow well in the damp soil along riverbanks. They have strong **roots** to hold them up.

willow tree

Tree roots hold the soil on riverbanks in place and stop it from being washed away by the water.

Riverbank animals

Look over there at the edge of the riverbank.
A **grebe** has made a nest among the reeds.

UP CLOSE

If you see a grebe on the water, watch carefully to see it diving down for fish. Grebes are brilliant at swimming underwater.

nest

Otters live in holes or hollow logs near
the edge of the water.

strong tail

webbed feet

Like grebes, otters are excellent swimmers and
they feed on fish. They have **webbed feet** and
strong tails to help them move faster in the water.

A waterside home

Who made this hole in the riverbank?

burrow entrance

It was a water vole. Voles dig homes
called **burrows** in steep riverbanks.

Look, the vole has come out of its burrow to feed. Voles eat plants that grow near the water.

UP CLOSE

You may think voles look a bit like rats. But unlike rats, they have round faces and furry ears.

River birds

What was that sudden flash of blue?

It was a kingfisher landing on its **perch**. It is about to swallow a fish!

UP CLOSE

If you are by a stretch of clear, slow-flowing water, you may see a kingfisher sitting on a perch. Watch it dive into the water and return with a fish!

Did you hear a splashing sound?
A swan is landing on the water.

Swans are one of the heaviest flying birds. They
find it easier to land on water than to take off!

Fish and frogs

There is a **shoal** of small fish swimming among the plants. What kind of fish are they?

They are minnows. Minnows like to swim in large groups.

Did you hear a 'plopping' sound? A frog has just jumped into the water. There it is among the lilies.

UP CLOSE

Frogs like damp places and can often be spotted in or near slow-moving rivers. In spring, they lay their eggs in still water at the edges of ponds or lakes.

River insects

Look at this insect darting to and fro, close to the surface of the water. It is a dragonfly.

You can often see dragonflies hunting insects near the water.

The water is shallow here. There is something crawling on the **riverbed**. It is a dragonfly **nymph**.

UP CLOSE

Dragonflies lay their eggs in the water. The eggs hatch into nymphs. They stay underwater until they are ready to change into adult dragonflies.

On the riverbed

What other creatures can we see on the riverbed?

This snail is feeding on weeds at the bottom of the river.

claw

This crayfish is crawling along the riverbed looking for food. Crayfish use their claws to catch snails and small fish.

UP CLOSE

Crayfish may be difficult to spot on the riverbed. They spend most of their time hiding among plants and under stones.

Through the year

A river is a good place to look for wildlife all through the year. If you visit often, you will see how the wildlife **adapts** to the changing seasons.

Spring

Spring is the season of new growth and new life. Look out for buds and flowers on trees. You may also see nests on the riverbank and water birds with their young.

Summer

In summer, wild flowers bloom on riverbanks and the air buzzes with the sound of insects.

Autumn

In autumn, many trees lose their leaves. Look for **fungi** and small creatures among the fallen leaves on the riverbank.

Winter

Winter is a good time to spot birds by the river, including pintail ducks and other birds that visit for the winter.

Be a nature detective

When you go for a nature walk by the river, be a nature detective and look for these things:

Otter footprints

Look out for animal tracks in the soft mud by the edge of riverbanks. Can you work out which type of animal has been there?

Mink

Look out for holes in the bank and for hollow logs. They may be a clue that an animal is nearby. Mink often make their homes in hollow logs near the water.

Herons' nests

As well as looking close to the ground, look for wildlife in the air and in the trees. Herons often make their nests high up in the branches by the riverbank.

Dragonfly laying eggs

When you spot an insect by the river, watch to see what it is doing. Is it looking for food? If you see a dragonfly, it may be about to lay its eggs in the water.

Scented flowers

When you see wild flowers growing by the river, look closely at their colour and size, and the shape of their petals and leaves. Do they have a smell?

Nature walk tips

As you walk along the riverbank, be as quiet as possible. Walk slowly, listen carefully and look all around you. Try not to disturb the wildlife you find. It is important not to touch eggs in nests or pick wild flowers.

Take a notepad and pencil with you and make notes about the animals and plants you see or draw sketches of them. Then you can look them up and find out more about them at home or at school.

If you have a camera, take it with you so you can photograph the animals and plants you see.

Binoculars will help you spot wild-life in the distance.

Glossary

adapt   to change to become more suited to a habitat

burrow   a hole in the ground dug by an animal to live in

fronds   the leaves of plants such as ferns

fungi   mushrooms and toadstools

grebe   a bird that lives by water

habitat   the home of a group of animals and plants

hatch   to be born from an egg

mallard   a type of duck

nymph   the young form of some insects, such as dragonflies

perch   a bird's resting place

reed   a tall plant that grows in or near water

riverbank   the side edges of the river

riverbed   the bottom of a river

roots   the parts of a plant that grow down into the soil

shoal   a group of fish that swim together

webbed feet   feet with skin between the toes or claws

Index